Keith Waterhouse and W

WORZEL GUMMIDGE GOES TO THE SEASIDE

Based on characters created by Barbara Euphan Todd

Photographs by Barry Rickman and Tony Nutley

PUFFIN BOOKS

PUFFIN BOOKS

Published by the Penguin Group
27 Wrights Lane, London W8 5TZ, England
Viking Penguin Inc., 40 West 23rd Street, New York, New York 10010, USA
Penguin Books Australia Ltd, Ringwood, Victoria, Australia
Penguin Books Canada Ltd, 2801 John Street, Markham, Ontario, Canada L3R 1B4
Penguin Books (N.Z.) Ltd, 182–190 Wairau Road, Auckland 10, New Zealand

Penguin Books Ltd, Registered Offices: Harmondsworth, Middlesex, England

Published in Puffin Books 1980
Reprinted 1983, 1985, 1988

Copyright © Waterhall Worzel Ltd, 1980
Photographs © Southern Television Ltd, 1980
All rights reserved

Made and printed in Italy

Except in the United States of America, this book is sold subject
to the condition that it shall not, by way of trade or otherwise, be lent,
re-sold, hired out, or otherwise circulated without the
publisher's prior consent in any form of binding or cover other than
that in which it is published and without a similar condition
including this condition being imposed on the subsequent purchaser

Worzel Gummidge stands in the middle of Ten-acre Field on a hot day.

Worzel is feeling hot and hungry. He wonders what to do about it.

A figure on a borrowed bicycle is soon pedalling along quickly in the direction of Mrs Bloomsbury-Barton's pond.

It's Worzel wearing his Wangling Head because he has decided to go fishing. But first he makes sure no one is around.

He tries Mrs Bloomsbury-Barton's pond. The water is nice and cool. He looks forward to catching a tasty fish. But Worzel has no luck. Perhaps nobody has ever told him that fish aren't very fond of carrots!

Worzel is soon rushing back to Ten-acre Field to meet John and Sue, full of wonderful stories of the fish he *nearly* caught.

John and Sue don't think much of his boasting. 'Won't he be surprised by our news', whispers Sue to John.
  They tell Worzel that all the grown-ups in the village are going to the seaside in a coach.
  'You can catch *huge* fish at the seaside', says John.

Worzel rushes off again excitedly but on his way, he meets Aunt Sally.

'Where do you think you're going?' she asks.

'I's goin' to the seaside, Aunt Sally,' says Worzel, 'an' I's goin' to bring you back a nice piece o' fish to eat. An' a stick o' rock.'

Before she can ask more, he hurries on.

Worzel changes quickly into his holiday clothes and gets out his bucket and spade. He watches the villagers getting into the coach.

'Excuse me, ma'am', he asks Mrs Braithwaite. 'Can I come to the seaside too?'

'Certainly not', answers Mrs Braithwaite. 'The trip is only for those who've paid.' Worzel is not pleased.

But Worzel has an idea. When nobody is looking, he creeps into the boot of the coach and travels down to the seaside that way.

Worzel arrives at the harbour of the seaside town. He looks around for somewhere to fish or build a sandcastle.

He notices somebody. It is a figurehead on a ship. Her name is Saucy Nancy but she doesn't look very happy.

Worzel climbs on the ship. He says hello and introduces himself to Saucy Nancy.

He and Saucy Nancy are soon good friends. She cheers up and Worzel asks her if she would like to take a walk round the harbour with him.

Saucy Nancy agrees happily although, being a figurehead, she's not very used to walking.

They are getting along fine and enjoying the seaside when Saucy Nancy suddenly gives a little scream.

Aunt Sally is sitting on a bench looking unhappy.
She has come down on the coach too, without Worzel
knowing, and now she wants her fish.
Worzel has to introduce her to Saucy Nancy. The
three of them go off together, although Aunt Sally
is not very pleased about this.

In the end, Worzel asks, 'What's the matter, Aunt Sally?'

'I thought you loved me,' she says, 'and came to the seaside just to get me some nice fish.'

Saucy Nancy isn't too happy either. In the park she asks Worzel to explain who Aunt Sally is.

'She's my fiancée,' says Worzel. 'We're going to be married.'

Saucy Nancy tells Worzel and Aunt Sally not to quarrel if they're engaged. 'I won't come between you,' she says.

Saucy Nancy goes back to the harbour and lets the Captain put her back on the front of his ship.

She doesn't look very pleased to be back but she knows she has done the right thing. Worzel tries to speak to her and to say good-bye but the Captain won't let him.

Worzel returns to Aunt Sally in the park.

'Well, where's the fish you promised me?' asks Aunt Sally.

'I don't know,' says Worzel, 'but how about tea an' cakes instead?'